Amy

Tips for Reading Together

Children learn best when reading is fun.

- Talk about the title and the pictures on the cover.
- Discuss what you think the story might be about.
- Read the story together, inviting your child to read as much of it as they can.
- Give lots of praise as your child reads, and help them when necessary.
- Try different ways of helping if they get stuck on a word. For example, get them to say the first sound of the word, or break it into chunks, or read the whole sentence again, trying to guess the word. Focus on the meaning.
- Re-read the story later, encouraging your child to read as much of it as they can.

Children enjoy re-reading stories and this helps to build their confidence.

Have fun!

The Stolen Crown
Part 2

Written by Roderick Hunt

Illustrated by Alex Brychta

OXFORD

UNIVERSITY PRESS

Read these words before you begin the story:

crown

prison

moat

search

castle

guards

magnifying

catch

jewel

other

arrow

untied

something

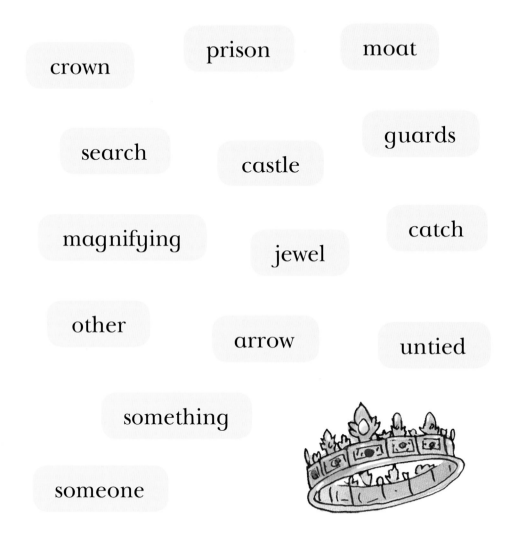

someone

Can you find the words in the story that rhyme with *crown*?

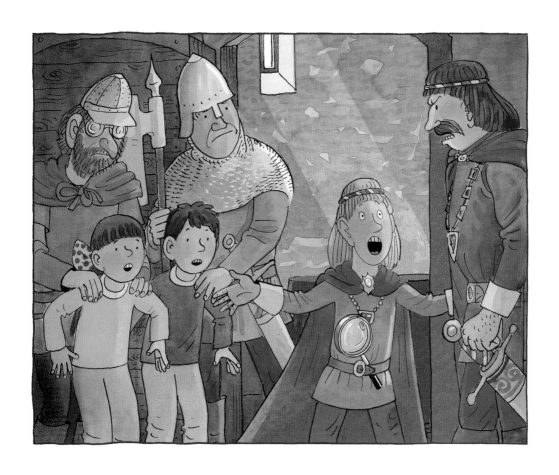

Have you read Part 1?

"These children stole the crown," said Lord Kent. "Throw them in prison."

"Stop!" said Henry. "I don't think they stole my crown."

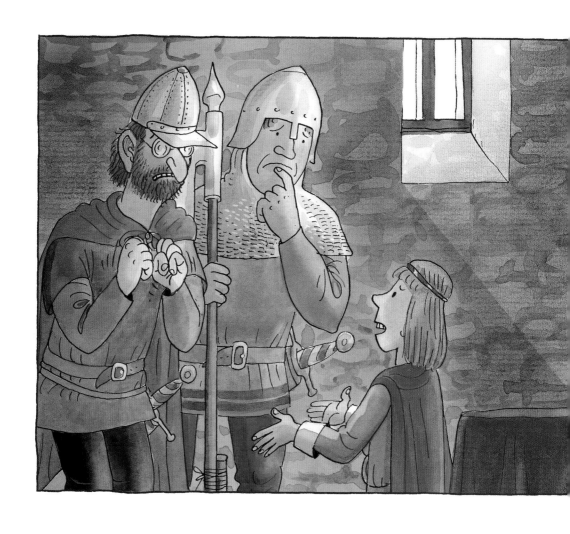

Henry spoke to the guards. "Who has
been in this room today?" he asked.

"You and Lord Kent," said a guard.

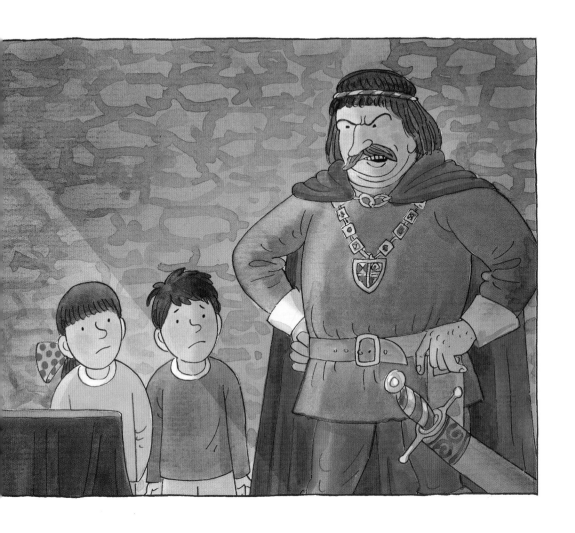

"Nobody could have taken it out of this room," said the other guard. "We search everyone."

"The children took it," said Lord Kent.

"We didn't take it," said Biff, "and
nobody else could get in from the
outside."

Chip saw something on the floor. It
was a broken arrow. He asked Henry to
lend him the magnifying glass.

"Someone tied string to the window," said Chip. "I think I know how the crown was stolen."

"Someone was in this room. Then someone outside the castle shot an arrow through the window. It had string tied to it."

"The person in the room put the string through the crown. Then they tied the string round this bar in the window."

"The crown slid down the string. Then the person in the room untied the string and left. It was easy."

"I know who stole the crown," said
Henry. "You, Lord Kent. You want to
stop me being the king."

Suddenly, Lord Kent ran off.

"Ha!" he shouted. "You will not be
king. I will! You have lost the crown."

"Catch him!" shouted Henry. "Don't
let him get away."

Biff and Chip grabbed Lord Kent's
cloak and pulled him over.

"Throw him in prison!" shouted Henry.

Henry ran out of the castle.

"Come on!" he called to Biff and Chip.

"We have to get my crown back."

Suddenly, Henry stopped running.
Two men were searching for something
in the grass.

"Keep down," hissed Henry. "Don't let them see us."

"What are they looking for?" asked Biff.

One man took the crown out of a bag.

"This is bad news," he said. "The biggest jewel in the crown is missing."

"We must find it," said the other man.
"Lord Kent will think we have stolen it."

"It must be here," said the first man. "I
hope it didn't fall in the moat."

Chip had an idea. In his pocket was a glass bead.

"Is this the jewel?" he asked.

"No," said Henry. "The jewel is much bigger."

"Give Biff the magnifying glass, Henry," said Chip, "and stay where you are."

Biff and Chip went up to the men.

Biff held the magnifying glass over the bead.

"Are you looking for this big jewel?" she said. "We have just found it."

Suddenly, Biff dropped the bead.
The men bent down to get it. She
grabbed the crown and Chip pushed
the men into the moat. Splash!

Biff threw the crown to Henry.

"Don't drop it!" yelled Chip. "Now run!
You can be king after all!"

"I'm glad I'm not a king," said Chip.
"You just can't trust anyone."

"But you can trust the magic key,"
said Biff. "It's glowing."

"Henry was just a boy," said Chip. "I wonder if he was king for a long time?"

"Who knows?" said Biff. "I wonder if he found that missing jewel?"

Think about the story

How did the men get the crown?

What was missing from the crown?

Why did Lord Kent want to steal the crown?

How do you think you would feel if you were a young king like Henry?

Spot the difference

Find 10 differences.

Useful common words repeated in this story and other books in the series:

these nobody everyone outside could through suddenly shouted catch don't stopped wonder what

Names in the story: Biff Chip Henry Lord Kent

More books for you to enjoy

Level 1:
Getting Ready

Level 2:
Atarting to Read

Level 3:
Becoming a Reader

Level 4:
Building Confidence

Level 5:
Reading with Confidence

OXFORD
UNIVERSITY PRESS

Great Clarendon Street,
Oxford OX2 6DP

Text © Roderick Hunt 2007
Illustrations © Alex Brychta 2007

First published 2007

This edition published 2110
All rights reserved

Read at Home Series Editors:
Kate Ruttle, Annemarie Young

British Library Cataloguing
in Publication Data available

ISBN: 9780198387794

10 9 8 7 6 5 4 3 2 1

Printed in China by Imago

Have more fun with Read at Home